# AT THE MOVIES

## HUMAN RESOURCE MANAGEMENT

**JOSEPH E. CHAMPOUX**
THE ROBERT O. ANDERSON SCHOOLS OF MANAGEMENT
THE UNIVERSITY OF NEW MEXICO

**THOMSON**

**SOUTH-WESTERN**

Australia · Canada · Mexico · Singapore · Spain · United Kingdom · United States

*To my former students, worldwide, who have enjoyed learning with film.*

# Preface

Films offer a rich resource for learning Human Resource management principles, theories, concepts, and issues. This resource of over a century of filmmaking is readily available on VHS videotape and increasingly on DVD. It ranges from such classics as *Breakfast at Tiffany's* (1961)—a film that offers a view of customer service—to contemporary films such as *Rush Hour 2* (2001)—an entertaining film that has glimpses of Hong Kong culture. Animated films, which have enjoyed a renaissance with computer graphics technology, also offer learning resources. *Antz* (1998), for example, has wonderful opening scenes showing many aspects of work, organizations, management, and Human Resource management issues.

This book is the product of my on-going cinema-based research and cinema-based teaching. I have found that students respond positively to the link between film scenes and abstract theories and concepts. Film offers a visualization of Human Resource management concepts that often are abstract in textbooks and lectures. For example, one can read about selection and placement. A visualization of selection and placement with a carefully chosen film scene can reinforce it dramatically. *Bowfinger* (1999) has an early scene showing these two Human Resource management topics. Bobby Bowfinger (Steve Martin) needs a lookalike for expensive film star Kit Ramsey (Eddie Murphy). He interviews Kit's brother Jiff Ramsey (also Eddie Murphy), selects him, and places him in his first film assignment—cross a busy Los Angeles freeway. You likely will remember these hilarious scenes as a visual representation of selection and placement.

I have carefully viewed and selected film scenes that show Human Resource management principles, concepts, and issues—and entertain—mining what I think is the rich trove of world cinema to compile this book. I designed it as a supplement for Human Resource management courses. The order of its thirty-two scenes is about the same as most popular Human Resource management textbooks. This order should let you and your instructor easily align the film scenes and their themes with your course's main text.

This book has two parts. Part I, "Film As a Learning Resource," describes the unique aspects of film that make it a powerful learning resource. Read this part first before beginning to use film in your learning program.

Part II, "Film Scenes for Learning Human Resource Management Principles, Theories, and Concepts" has film and scene descriptions for thirty-two topics. I present the film scene for each topic in a convenient two-page format. The left page describes the film and the scene; the right page has space for your name, your analysis, and personal reactions.

Each scene discussion includes film and scene descriptions, and a list of questions and issues to think about and watch for while viewing the scene. There is also a list of concepts or examples. If these concepts or examples appear in the scene, you can check them off when you see them. Marking them as you see them will help when writing your analysis.

I give approximate scene starting and stopping points so you can quickly find the scene on the referenced VHS videotape in the National Television Standards Committee (NTSC) format or DVD in Area 1 format.* I also give approximate scene running times to help you manage your classroom and independent study time. These estimates are specific to the distributor of the videotape or DVD shown under the film title.

You can use VHS videotapes or DVDs from a different distributor or in other formats. The starting points for different distributors and formats can differ from those shown for the scenes in this text. Scene descriptions have enough detail to let you find the scene on a videotape or DVD of any format. The descriptions use a "bracketing" technique, describing what occurs before and after the scene. This method will help you find the scene quickly, especially if you are unfamiliar with the film. The introduction to Part II has more details on scene start and stop points for VHS videotapes and DVDs. I suggest you read that introduction before trying to locate and view scenes.

You can use this book in different ways. Your instructor might show the scene in class for class discussion. Or, your instructor may assign scenes for your out-of-class viewing as an individual or in small groups. He or she may want you to write your analysis and turn it in for class credit.

You can also use film scenes in this book for individual or group presentations in other classes. For example, the workforce diversity scenes (Scene 3) will work well in presentations for an Organizational Behavior class. Using film scenes in such presentations can enliven them and help you make your points effectively.

This book also works well for independent study. All films in this book are available for rent from video stores and other sources, such as public libraries. You can supplement your reading and other studying by viewing scenes linked to topics you are trying to learn.

I based the film descriptions in this book on the latest versions of the following film reference sources:

- *Leonard Maltin's Movie & Video Guide*
- *The Seventh Virgin Film Guide*
- *VideoHound's DVD Guide, Books 1–3*
- *VideoHound's Golden Movie Retriever*

I also used the Internet Movie Database *(http://www.imdb.com)* and different film studies resources referenced throughout this book.

You may enjoy learning more about a specific film. I suggest using the reference books mentioned and the Internet Movie Database. This site has news about new and older films—and lets you search for specific film information. It also has message boards where you can chat with other people about films.

---

*See M. Long, DVD Regional Codes. In M. Mayo, ed., *VideoHound's DVD Guide, Book 3*, 2003, pp. xvii–xviii for a discussion of DVD format differences and different television standards.

The Web site *http://champoux.swcollege.com* has helpful documents such as "Cinema Resources on the World Wide Web," an extensive collection of useful and fun cinema Web Sites. I will regularly update this site to include other helpful sources for learning with film. The site also will have updates for the films in *At the Movies: Human Resource Management*. Descriptions of new film scenes that complement this book will also be available to enhance your learning.

I have used many film scenes described in this book in my undergraduate, Masters of Business Administration (MBA), and Executive MBA classes. I also have used many scenes with classes that I have taught in countries outside the United States. As a result, students and colleagues have recommended many scenes in this book for which they receive recognition. To all of you, I extend my greatest thanks for your positive responses and continual support. And it is to all of you that I have dedicated this work.

I also thank Libby Shipp, my production editor at South-Western, for keeping me well focused. Special thanks go to John Szilagyi, my executive editor, for continually seeing the value of my cinema-based projects.

An effort such as this workbook is always a "work-in-progress." I would enjoy feedback about any aspect of its content and design. Please send your comments and observations to me at the Robert O. Anderson Schools of Management, University of New Mexico, Albuquerque, New Mexico, 87131 USA. You can also send E-mail to *champoux@unm.edu*.

Joseph E. Champoux
Albuquerque, New Mexico, USA

# C o n t e n t s

# Film as a Learning Resource[*]

Videotaped films are now widely available for inexpensive rental or purchase, making them an accessible learning resource. Films now available from a video store include contemporary films, classical films, foreign films, documentaries, and some television series. About 24,000 such films are available on videotape, laserdisc, and DVD (Craddock 2002; Maltin 2002; Martin and Porter 2002).

Film scenes offer a visual portrayal of abstract theories and concepts discussed in typical Human Resource management books and taught in related courses. Viewing concepts through different film scenes also shows the application of these concepts in different situations.

I refer to specific film scenes at several points as examples of the observation discussed. The source article in the footnote for this summary discusses those scenes in more detail.

## Film Theory

A review of the film theory and the film studies literature suggested some unique features of film that make it an uncommonly powerful learning tool. An early film theorist, Siegfried Kracauer, captured this view of film when he said: "[A unique property of film is its ability to] make one see and grasp things which only the cinema is privileged to communicate" (Kracauer 1973, x).

Some unique aspects of film and film making let this medium show Human Resource management principles and concepts in an uncommonly powerful way. Understanding these aspects of film will help you understand the examples of scenes discussed later and throughout this book.

---

[*]*Source:* Adapted from Joseph E. Champoux, "Film as a Teaching Resource." *Journal of Management Inquiry*, Vol. 8, No. 2 (June 1999): 206–217 © 1999 Sage Publications, Inc. Reprinted by permission of Sage Publications, Inc. See this article for a more detailed description and full citations for this summary on learning with film.

## Film Characteristics

Film records physical reality but sees it differently from ordinary human experiences (Andrew 1984; Arnheim 1957). Film is unequaled in its ability to hold and direct the attention of the viewer. Lens techniques, focusing techniques, camera movements, camera angles, framing of shots, and film editing can create gripping views not found in reality (Carroll 1985). The following summarizes these major film characteristics.

- **Close-up shot**: Lets a director show a viewer something that might go unnoticed with ordinary vision. Example: *12 Angry Men*
- **Long shot**: Shows the viewer more than what ordinary vision shows. Example: *Broadcast News*
- **Deep focus**: All parts of a scene are in focus from the nearest object to the farthest. Example: *The Hudsucker Proxy*
- **Soft focus**: Keeps objects nearest the viewer in focus; puts objects farther away out of focus. Example: *Top Gun*
- **Film editing**: Puts a series of images together in a unique sequence intended to have specific effects on the viewer. Example: *The Godfather*
- **Shot/reverse-shot**: Shows social interaction between two or more parties; scene switches from a view of one party to a view of the other party in the conversation. Example: *Broadcast News*
- **Sound, dialogue**: Delivery of dialogue by the actor or actress adds to the drama, humor, or satire of a scene. Example: *Head Office*
- **Sound, composed music**: Deliberately controlled in tempo, loudness, and color to give desired effects to the cinematic experience. Example: *Top Gun*
- **Sound, music taken from other sources**: Often has meaning for viewers from earlier exposure to the music; lets a director use borrowed music as a satirical device or emphasize meaning to certain film themes. Example: *2001: A Space Odyssey*
- **Special effects**: Enhancements that come from many sources; computer effects are increasingly common in modern films. Example: *Metropolis*

## Viewer Responses

Viewers are not passive observers of images on a screen. They can have many different responses, some of which come from film's unique features (Allbritton and Gerrig 1991; Gerrig and Prentice 1996). Viewer responses often become an essential part of the film experience.

The shot/reverse-shot editing technique described earlier creates a viewing experience that does not happen in the real world. A viewer can see all aspects of the conversation the director considers important to the film's story. Nonverbal cues from eye movement, facial expression, and body movement can load images with information a viewer interprets. Directors can embed these scenes with high emotional, satirical, or comical content that a viewer can only experience with the film medium.

## Media, Cognition, and Learning

Traditional learning media include lecture/discussion and printed media such as book materials or projected text. Visual forms include overhead projection of drawings, slide projection of images, or computer projection of slides. I recommend adding film and film scenes to existing learning and instructional media. Several lines of research suggest different learning effects of different media forms. The conclusion from both brain and media and cognition research points compellingly to using multi-media for learning.

## Learning Functions of Film

Films can serve many learning functions. The functions that will work for you depend on your learning style and learning goals. The following is an overview of ways of using film as case, metaphor, satire, symbolism, meaning, experience, and time.

- **Film as Case**: Case analysis is an obvious use of film and perhaps the first that one thinks of when considering film for learning. Scenes from a well-acted and well-directed film present material more dramatically and engagingly than a print case. Example: *The Coca-Cola Kid*
- **Film as Metaphor**: Metaphors serve many functions in prose and poetry and can serve similar functions when using film for learning (Cooper 1986; Hawkes 1972; Mooij 1976). Metaphors often leave lasting impressions that a person easily recalls. Example: *Scent of a Woman*
- **Film as Satire**: Satire is an effective art form for burning concepts into a person's mind (Feinberg 1967; Griffin 1994, 1; Test 1991). It uses humor and ridicule to contrast pretense and reality. Well-done satire can leave an unforgettable image of concepts you are trying to learn. Example: *Modern Times*
- **Film as Symbolism**: Some scenes from films can offer a symbolic way of communicating theories and concepts. Unusual shots, sequencing, lighting, and the use of black and white film often convey symbolism. Example: *Ikiru (to Live)*
- **Film as Meaning**: Film is an excellent medium for giving meaning to theories and concepts. The visual and auditory effects of great films can convey a message better than printed or spoken words. Example: *12 Angry Men*
- **Film as Experience**: The unique qualities of film described earlier can create strong experiences for viewers (Stadler 1990). You can use this feature of film to introduce yourself to other countries' cultures. Example: *Ciao, Professore!*

- **Film as Time**: Films portraying earlier periods can help show aspects of management and management behavior during an earlier time. Example: *Tucker: The Man and His Dream*

## Ways of Using Film for Learning

There are several ways of using film for learning Human Resource management principles, theories, and concepts (Proctor and Adler 1991; Zorn 1991). Experimenting with each method will show you which ones are most effective for your learning style and course content.

- **Before:** Viewing film scenes before reading or studying can give you a recallable visual image to which you can compare the topics you are studying. This approach allows quick reference to easily recallable examples shown in the film. Example: *Top Gun*
- **After:** Viewing scenes after reading or studying theories and concepts lets you use the scenes as a video case. This approach helps develop your analytical skills in applying what you are learning. Example: *Top Gun*
- **Repeat:** Repeating scenes is especially helpful when trying to develop your understanding of complex topics (Wolensky 1982). View the scenes before studying concepts to give you a visual anchor. Rerun the scenes to analyze them with the concepts you have studied. Example: *The Firm*
- **Comparison:** Films offer rich opportunities for comparisons in several ways. Remakes of the same film can offer a chance to see the same culture at different times. Example: *Sabrina* (1954); *Sabrina* (1995)

## Summary

Film and film scenes are a widely available, easily accessed, learning resource. Many unique characteristics of film as a communication medium give it especially positive effects on learning. You can use film in different ways to enhance your learning: as case, metaphor, satire, symbolism, or experience. You also can align film scenes in different ways in your studying program. Try the film scenes in this book as enhancers for your study of Human Resource management principles, concepts, and theories. You will surprise yourself about how much film can improve your learning and retention.

# Film Scenes for Learning Human Resource Management Principles, Theories, and Concepts

Part II has film and scene descriptions for thirty-two Human Resource management topics. Each scene description has location information for both DVD and VHS videotape. Location information format and interpretation differ for the two formats.

The format for **DVD scene positions** varies, depending on whether a scene is an entire chapter, entire multiple chapters, part of a chapter, or part of multiple chapters.* The following describes the format of each possibility:

- **Entire single chapter:** Chapter number and chapter title.
- **Entire multiple chapters:** Chapter numbers and chapter titles linked by the word "through."
- **Part of single chapter:** Chapter number and chapter title, followed by "(Start: 0:00:00)" for the scene's beginning or "(Stop: 0:00:00)" for the scene's end. The numbers show the start and stop positions in a chapter. This format also is used for multiple chapters. Start and stop positions within a single chapter appear as "(Start: 0:00:00 — Stop: 0:00:00)."
- **Part of multiple chapters:** Chapter numbers and chapter titles linked by the word "to." Start and stop positions within the beginning and ending chapters noted as shown above for "Part of chapter."

**VHS videotape scene position** information is the same throughout Part II. It always appears as "(Start: 0:00:00 — Stop: 0:00:00 — 0 minutes)." The last entry shows the scene elapsed time, which also applies to the DVD.

Scene position description information applies to the noted distributor of a film's DVD and VHS videotape. See the "Preface" (pp. *v-vi*) for more information about the "bracketing" technique used to describe scene positions.

---

*A DVD's main menu often uses a phrase similar to "Scene Selection" to refer to where you select chapters. Whatever phrase used in a menu refers to chapters.

# Antz

Color, 1998
Running Time: 1 hour, 23 minutes
Rating: PG
Director: Eric Darnell, Tim Johnson
Distributor: *DreamWorks Home Entertainment*

Z (voiced by Woody Allen) is an insignificant worker ant in a massive ant colony. He is trying to find his role in life and pursue Princess Bala (voiced by Sharon Stone). Everything changes after he trades places with Weaver (voiced by Sylvester Stallone), his soldier ant friend. A termite war and the pursuit of the evil General Mandible (voiced by Gene Hackman) take Z's life to new and unexpected places. This DreamWorks production is a wonderful example of modern computer animation.[*]

## Scenes

- **DVD: Chapter 1, Insignificantz (Main Titles) (Start: 0:00:52) to Chapter 2, The General's Plan (Stop: 0:08:00)**
- **VHS: (Start: 0:04:11 — Stop: 0:11:21 — 7 minutes)**

These scenes start after the opening credits with a shot of the New York City skyline. Z's voice-over says, "All my life I've lived and worked in the big city." They end as General Mandible and Colonel Cutter (voiced by Christopher Walken) leave to meet the Queen. Mandible says, "Our very next stop, Cutter." The film cuts to the meeting between the Queen (voiced by Anne Bancroft) and General Mandible.

## What to Watch for and Ask Yourself

- What major work-related issues do these scenes raise? How are they related to Human Resource (HR) management?
- Do you now see, or have you seen, these issues in your work experiences?
- What services would HR management offer to the supervisors and workers of this ant colony organization?

---

[*]Originally suggested by Greg McNeil, undergraduate student, The Robert O. Anderson School of Management, The University of New Mexico. — J.E.C.

## Concepts or Examples

☐ Personal needs

☐ Meaningful work

☐ Supervisory behavior

☐ HR: job redesign

☐ Worker contribution to the larger organization

☐ Theory X assumptions

☐ Theory Y assumptions

☐ HR: supervisory training

## Analysis

_____

_____

_____

_____

_____

_____

## Personal Reactions

_____

_____

_____

_____

# Office Space

Color, 1999
Running Time: 1 hour, 39 minutes
Rating: R
Director: Mike Judge
Distributor: *20th Century Fox Home Entertainment*

This biting satire looks at modern American corporate life through the eyes of three computer programmers. Peter Gibbons (Ron Livingston) is a computer programmer with less than positive feelings about his company, Initech. He and his co-workers develop a way of getting back at the company. This film is director Mike Judge's live-action debut. He is the creator of the television series *Beavis and Butthead* (Craddock 2002, 556).

Office Space features a red Swingline® stapler, a favorite of the character Milton (Stephen Root). At the time of the film's making, Swingline did not manufacture a red stapler. A prop designer custom painted a stapler for the film, leading to an almost cult-like following for that color. Early in 2002, Swingline introduced its Rio Red stapler, but only through its Website (Fowler 2002). A defining moment for Milton's relationship with his beloved stapler appears early in the film.*

## Scenes

- **DVD: Chapter 1, Road Rage (Start: 0:00:25) to Chapter 3, A Case of the Mondays (Stop: 00:08:11)**
- **VHS: (Start: 0:06:55 — Stop: 0:14:41 — 8 minutes)**

This sequence begins the film following the black title screen, "Twentieth Century Fox Presents." It starts with a shot of a crowded highway during morning rush hour traffic. It ends after Peggy (Barbara George-Reiss) says, "Uh-oh. Sounds like somebody's got a case of the Mondays." Peter stares at Samir (Ajay Naidu) and Michael (David Herman). The film cuts to the three programmers having coffee at Chotchkie's. (Some R-rated language occurs early in these scenes.)

## What to Watch for and Ask Yourself

- Does Peter have negative attitudes about working at Initech? Why?
- Does this workforce composition appear typical of present day organizations?
- What challenges face Intech HR professionals?

---

*DVD Chapter 11, The Red Stapler; VHS: (Start: 0:39:14 — Stop: 0:40:31 — 1 minute)

## Concepts or Examples

- ☐ Work attitudes
- ☐ Organizational commitment
- ☐ Job satisfaction
- ☐ Diverse workforce

- ☐ Supervisory satisfaction
- ☐ Job involvement
- ☐ HR challenges

## Analysis

_____

_____

_____

_____

_____

_____

## Personal Reactions

_____

_____

_____

_____

_____

# Babe

Color, 1995
Running Time: 1 hour, 32 minutes
Rating: G
Director: Chris Noonan
Distributor: *Universal Studios Home Video*

A charming Australian film featuring eccentric, quiet Farmer Hoggett (James Cromwell) who trains a pig he won at the fair to herd his sheep. His eccentricity turns to determination when he enters the pig in the Australian National Sheepdog Championships. The Academy Award-winning visual effects include a seamless mixture of animatronic doubles, computer images, and live animals.[*]

## Scenes

- **DVD: Chapter 8, a pig that thinks it's a dog
  (Start: 0:38:17 — Stop: 0:44:35)**
- **VHS: (Start: 0:44:03 — Stop: 0:50:20 — 6 minutes)**

These scenes start with Hoggett opening his new motor-powered gate and calling his dogs and Babe (voiced by Christine Cavanaugh). Hoggett says, "Come Rex. Come Fly. Come Pig." They follow the scene of Hoggett noticing that Babe sorted some chickens by their color. The scenes end as a horse-drawn wagon goes down a hill. Fly (voiced by Miriam Margolyes) says to Babe, "No, no, now. I think you better leave that to me." The film fades to a shot of the moon. The sheep call the dogs "wolves."

## What to Watch for and Ask Yourself

- Are Babe's methods of herding sheep different from those used by sheepdogs? If *yes*, what are the differences?
- Does Babe discover that he cannot successfully herd sheep as a sheep dog herds them? What does he do?
- Does Farmer Hoggett accept Babe for what he is—a pig not a sheep dog?

---

[*]Film and scene descriptions adapted from J. E. Champoux, Seeing and Valuing Diversity Through Film, *Educational Media International* 36 (December 1999): 310–316. © Taylor & Francis Ltd., P. O. Box 25, Abingdon, Oxfordshire, OX14 3UE. Reprinted by permission.

## Concepts or Examples

- ☐ Diversity
- ☐ Different behaviors reach the same goal
- ☐ Cannot change who you are
- ☐ Dimensions of diversity

- ☐ Rejection of differences
- ☐ Managing diversity
- ☐ Valuing diversity
- ☐ Diversity and performance
- ☐ Acceptance of differences

## Analysis

_____

_____

_____

_____

_____

## Personal Reactions

_____

_____

_____

_____

# Breakfast at Tiffany's

Color, 1961
Running Time: 1 hour, 54 minutes
Rating: NR
Director: Blake Edwards
Distributor: *Paramount Home Video*

An endearing Truman Capote story about Holly Golightly (Audrey Hepburn), a young rural woman who becomes a New York playgirl. She has a shaky romance with writer Paul Varjak (George Peppard). Although now almost a period film of mid-20th century New York life, the comedy and charming romance come through for any audience. The film features Henry Mancini's Academy Award winning song, "Moon River." In 2002, the American Film Institute ranked *Breakfast at Tiffany's* among the top 100 cinema love stories (Germain 2002).

## Scene

- **DVD: Chapter 10, Things We've Never Done**
  **(Start: 1:08:08 — Stop: 1:13:16)**
- **VHS: (Start: 1:11:45 — Stop: 1:16:22 — 5 minutes)**[*]

This scene starts with Paul and Holly walking along a Manhattan street. It follows the scene of Paul opening champagne in Holly's apartment. The scene ends after Holly kisses the Tiffany's sales clerk (John MacGiver) and says, "Didn't I tell you this is a lovely place." The film dissolves to Paul and Holly looking into a store window. They continue their Manhattan stroll and go to the public library so Holly can sit and rest.[†]

## What to Watch for and Ask Yourself

- Does the Tiffany's sales clerk focus on the needs and desires of Paul and Holly?
- Is he flexible in his response to their request? What does he do to meet their budget requirements?
- Would you expect this type of customer service in a modern, upscale jewelry store?

---

[*]VHS videotape scene position information applies to "The Audrey Hepburn Collection" release of the film with a 2001 copyright on the videotape box. The scene's position on older videotapes is (Start: 1:08:40 — Stop: 1:13:16 — 5 minutes).

[†]Originally suggested by Elizabeth McCormick, Olivia Timmons, and Jeff Loafman, undergraduate students, The Robert O. Anderson School of Management, The University of New Mexico. — J.E.C.

## Concepts or Examples

☐ Quality management         ☐ Flexible response

☐ Customer service           ☐ Inflexible response

☐ Customer focus              ☐ Customer needs and desires

## Analysis

_____

_____

_____

_____

_____

## Personal Reactions

_____

_____

_____

_____

# Rush Hour 2

Color, 2001
Running Time: 1 hour, 31 minutes
Rating: PG-13
Director: Brett Ratner
Distributor: *New Line Home Entertainment*

Hong Kong Chief Inspector Lee (Jackie Chan) and Los Angeles Detective Carter (Chris Tucker) are in Hong Kong for the vacation they began at the end of *Rush Hour* (1998). A bomb explosion in the American Consulate interrupts their plans almost immediately. Martial arts action reins in the hands of Jackie Chan and beautifully enhanced by opponent Hu Li (Ziyi Zhang of *Crouching Tiger, Hidden Dragon*, 2000). The banter between Lee and Carter offers almost non-stop humor.

## Scenes

- **DVD: Chapter 1, Main Titles / Deadly Delivery (Start: 0:00:16)**
- **VHS: (Start: 0:07:10 — Stop: 0:11:27 — 4 minutes)**

These scenes begin the film and include the opening credits. They follow the New Line Cinema logo. The camera pans to the top of a mountain, becoming an aerial shot of Hong Kong. These scenes end while Lee and Carter are driving through Hong Kong. Lee receives his assignment from his superintendent. He tells Carter they are going to a big party. The film cuts to the Triad Club.

## What to Watch for and Ask Yourself

- What do you immediately notice about modern Hong Kong from this cinema introduction?
- Does Carter show cultural sensitivity?
- Does it appear that Carter had any pre-departure cultural orientation or training before arriving in Hong Kong?

## Concepts or Examples

- ☐ Culture introduction
- ☐ Entering a foreign culture
- ☐ Cultural sensitivity

- ☐ Cultural insensitivity
- ☐ Cross-cultural preparation
- ☐ Pre-departure orientation and training

## Analysis

_____

_____

_____

_____

_____

_____

## Personal Reactions

_____

_____

_____

_____

_____

# You've Got Mail (I)

Color, 1998
Running Time: 2 hours
Rating: PG
Director: Nora Ephron
Distributor: *Warner Home Video*

Neighborhood bookstore owner Kathleen Kelly (Meg Ryan) regularly interacts over the Internet with book superstore head Joe Fox (Tom Hanks). The anonymity of Internet interactions disguises their identities. Kathleen eventually meets Joe Fox, but does not know he is the same person in her Internet interactions. Joe also does not know that Kathleen is his Internet partner. A charming, warm remake of the 1940 film *The Shop Around the Corner* (Craddock 2002, 848), in which the technology for interaction was letters by mail. See page 18 for another scene description.

## Scenes

- **DVD: Chapter 2, Morning log-ons (Start: 0:03:34) to Chapter 4, Cyber-romantics (Stop: 0:08:40)**
- **VHS: (Start: 0:04:34 — Stop: 0:09:39 — 5 minutes)**

Two sets of scenes offer strong contrasts in social interaction. This first set shows Internet interaction. The second set of scenes [*You've Got Mail* (II), pages 18–19] shows face-to-face interaction. Try to predict their face-to-face interaction before watching the second set of scenes.

The first scenes appear early in the film after the opening credits. Frank Navasky (Greg Kinnear) and Kathleen begin their day. He leaves for work. Kathleen comes out of the bathroom and logs on to America Online. These scenes end as Joe Fox approaches a shrouded building—the site of his new superstore. The film cuts to the store's interior with Joe discussing construction status with Kevin Jackson (Dave Chappelle).

## What to Watch for and Ask Yourself

- What effect does anonymity have on Kathleen and Joe's Internet interactions?
- Do you expect their face-to-face interaction to differ? Why and how?
- Can anonymous Internet interactions have similar effects in organizations?

## Concepts or Examples

☐ Verbal communication       ☐ Anonymity

☐ Internet interaction       ☐ Face-to-face interaction

☐ Nonverbal communication       ☐ Lack of anonymity

☐ Behavioral reactions

## Analysis

_____

_____

_____

_____

_____

_____

## Personal Reactions

_____

_____

_____

_____

_____

# You've Got Mail (II)

Color, 1998
Running Time: 2 hours
Rating: PG
Director: Nora Ephron
Distributor: *Warner Home Video*

See page 16 for the film description and another scene description.

## Scenes

- **DVD: Chapter 10, Who's worried? (Start: 0:32:37) through Chapter 11, Party patter**
- **VHS: (Start: 0:33:35 — Stop: 0:39:23 — 6 minutes)**

These scenes follow discussions about the effect of the Fox superstore on the sales of Kathleen's shop. They start with Frank's (Greg Kinnear) voice-over saying, "A nut? She ... she called me a nut?" Frank and Kathleen (Meg Ryan) walk to a party in the evening while having a conversation. These scenes end as the two couples separate and Joe (Tom Hanks) says to Patricia Eden (Parker Posey), "Hey hon'. Have you ever had a caviar garnish?" The film cuts to Joe and Patricia preparing for bed. Patricia talks about Frank.

## What to Watch for and Ask Yourself

- Do Kathleen and Joe's face-to-face interactions differ from their Internet interactions? If *yes*, how do they differ?
- Could interactions of this type (Internet, face-to-face) happen outside the world of cinema?
- What differences between their face-to-face interactions, and their anonymous Internet interactions, contribute to their behavioral reactions to each other?

## Concepts or Examples

☐ Anonymity                    ☐ Lack of anonymity

☐ Internet interaction         ☐ Face-to-face interaction

☐ Nonverbal communication      ☐ Behavioral reactions

## Analysis

_____

_____

_____

_____

_____

## Personal Reactions

_____

_____

_____

_____

_____

# Grumpier Old Men

Color, 1995
Running Time: 1 hour, 41 minutes
Rating: PG-13
Director: Howard Deutch
Distributor: *Warner Home Video*

This sequel to *Grumpy Old Men* (1993) features the same two grumps: Max Goldman (Walter Matthau) and John Gustafson (Jack Lemmon). It is a light-hearted comedy showing the lifelong relationship of two next-door neighbors. They constantly argue and insult each other but are actually good friends, especially when fishing. Their lifelong goal: catch the biggest, most elusive catfish in the lake, Catfish Hunter.

## Scenes

- **DVD: Chapter 26, Something fishy to Chapter 27, Where he belongs (Stop: 1:30:15)**
- **VHS: (Start: 1:27:14 — Stop: 1:33:38 — 6 minutes)**

These scenes start with an outside shot of John's house. Everyone is preparing for Max's wedding. The scenes follow his marriage proposal to Maria (Sophia Loren). They end as Max realizes he and John are late for his wedding. They race the boat to shore and drive to the church. Max sings a verse from "Get Me to the Church on Time."

## What to Watch for and Ask Yourself

- Do Max and John behave ethically or unethically? Do they understand what they *ought* to do?
- Do they face ethical dilemmas? How many?
- What ethical guidelines do they use to decide a course of action?

## Concepts or Examples

☐ Ethical behavior        ☐ Ethical guidelines

☐ Ethical dilemmas        ☐ Unethical behavior

## Analysis

_____

_____

_____

_____

_____

_____

## Personal Reactions

_____

_____

_____

_____

# Joe Versus the Volcano (I)

Color, 1990
Running Time: 1 hour, 42 minutes
Rating: PG
Director: John Patrick Shanley
Distributor: *Warner Home Video*

"Once upon a time there was a guy named Joe who had a very lousy job..." This film's opening title screens give strong clues about a typical workday for Joe Banks (Tom Hanks). He has a bad job and perhaps an even worse work environment. Joe does not feel well. Joe learns from his doctor that he has a "brain cloud," a rare disease that will kill him in six months. He accepts millionaire Samuel Harvey Graynamore's (Lloyd Bridges) offer of a vacation on Waponi Woo, a South Sea Island where he will live like a king. The bad part of the vacation comes when he learns he must jump into a local volcano as part of an island ritual. See pages 24 and 26 for descriptions of other scenes from this film.

## Scenes

- **DVD: Chapter 1, Grinding/Credits. (Start: 0:00:32) through Chapter 2, What's the matter?**
- **VHS: (Start: 0:03:07 — Stop: 0:13:57 — 11 minutes)**

These scenes begin the film. They start with the title screen, "Once upon a time there was a guy named Joe." The scenes end after Joe puts his hands to his face and you hear the voice-over, "Mr. Banks? Mr. Banks?" The film cuts to Dr. Ellison's (Robert Stack) office where Joe learns he has a brain cloud. The early part of these scenes brim with cinematic reference to Fritz Lang's *Metropolis* (1927), his expressionist allegory about the oppressed working class (Jurkiewicz, 1990).

## What to Watch for and Ask Yourself

- What type of work attitudes do the workers have—positive or negative? What are the attitude objects?
- How satisfied is Joe Banks with his job, work context, and supervision?
- Assuming Joe has the option of quitting his job, what do you predict he will do in the future?

## Concepts or Examples

☐ Attitudes

☐ Work attitudes

☐ Negative work attitude

☐ Attitudes and behavior

☐ Positive work attitude

## Analysis

_____

_____

_____

_____

_____

_____

## Personal Reactions

_____

_____

_____

_____

_____

# Joe Versus the Volcano (II)

Color, 1990
Running Time: 1 hour, 42 minutes
Rating: PG
Director: John Patrick Shanley
Distributor: *Warner Home Video*

See page 22 for the film description. Other scene descriptions appear on pages 22 and 26.

## Scene

- **DVD: Chapter 5, Joe quits.**
- **VHS: (Start: 0:20:57 — Stop: 0:26:22 — 6 minutes)**

This scene begins as Joe approaches the office and enters. They follow his diagnosis of a brain cloud and leaving the Medical League Building. He has adjusted the daisy crushed in the opening scene by a woman's boot. The scene ends after Joe leaves the office. De De (Meg Ryan) smiles while saying, "Wow! What a change." The film cuts to Joe talking to De De in a restaurant. He asks, "Who am I?"

## What to Watch for and Ask Yourself

- Is Joe Banks showing uncharacteristically rebellious work behavior?
- Does he lash out at everyone equally? Does he have positive attitudes and feelings toward some co-workers?
- Assess Mr. Waturi's behavior from a Human Resource management perspective. What could he have done differently?

## Concepts or Examples

☐ Attitudes                              ☐ Attitudes and behavior

☐ Work attitudes                         ☐ Positive work attitude

☐ Negative work attitude                 ☐ Rebellion

## Analysis

_____

_____

_____

_____

_____

## Personal Reactions

_____

_____

_____

_____

# Joe Versus the Volcano (III)

Color, 1990
Running Time: 1 hour, 42 minutes
Rating: PG
Director: John Patrick Shanley
Distributor: *Warner Home Video*

See page 22 for the film description. Pages 22 and 24 have descriptions of other scenes from this film.

## Scene

- **DVD: Chapter 6, Feeling great.**
- **VHS: (Start: 0:26:23 — Stop: 0:27:57 — 2 minutes)**

This scene starts with Joe Banks (Tom Hanks) talking to De De (Meg Ryan) across a restaurant table. He asks, "Who am I?" The scene follows the scenes of Joe quitting his job. This scene ends after De De says, "I wish I was where you are, Joe." He says, "No you don't." The film continues with their restaurant date.

## What to Watch for and Ask Yourself

- Does Joe Banks have a more positive view of life compared to his attitudes in the earlier scenes? Why?
- Can you see a relationship between his work attitudes and his attitudes away from work (nonwork attitudes)?
- Does such a relationship or effect happen in the world of working? Why or why not?

## Concepts or Examples

- ☐ Attitudes
- ☐ Work attitudes
- ☐ Negative work attitude

- ☐ Attitudes and behavior
- ☐ Positive work attitude
- ☐ Nonwork attitudes

## Analysis

_____

_____

_____

_____

_____

## Personal Reactions

_____

_____

_____

_____

_____

# Mission Impossible (I)*

Color, 1996
Running Time: 1 hour, 50 minutes
Rating: PG-13
Director: Brian DePalma
Distributor: *Paramount Pictures Corporation*

This box office hit from director Brian DePalma, based on the popular 1960s' television series, has tension-building special effects. The plot moves from Prague to Washington to a high-speed helicopter-train chase across the French countryside. Top undercover agent Ethan Hunt (Tom Cruise) takes his crack team on a mission that fails and the death of almost all members. Believing they were ambushed, Hunt sets out on a nearly impossible mission to get a computer disk with identities of hundreds of double agents. See page 30 for another scene description from *Mission Impossible*.

## Scenes

- **DVD: Chapter 2, Good Morning Mr. Phelps (Start: 0:03:53) through Chapter 3, Golitsyn**
- **VHS: (Start: 0:09:54 — Stop: 0:32:46 — 23 minutes)**

These scenes start after the *Mission Impossible* title screen. Jim Phelps (Jon Voight) is aboard an airplane looking at his wife's picture. A flight attendant approaches and offers him a movie. The scenes end after Hunt says into the telephone, "You're in Prague?" Ketterige (Henry Czerny), his agency supervisor, replies, "One hour." The film fades to Hunt walking along a Prague street going to the Akvárium (Aquarium) restaurant.

## What to Watch for and Ask Yourself

- What are the elements of the team's strategic plan? How do they coordinate the plan's elements and team members?
- Does each team member have a specialized role? Do the members have the knowledge, skills, and abilities to carry out their roles?
- Are they prepared for changing circumstances during the operation?

---

*The Roman numeral in parentheses does not refer to the film's version. It denotes the first of two scenes from this version of *Mission Impossible*.

## Concepts or Examples

- ☐ Strategy
- ☐ Strategic planning
- ☐ External environment
- ☐ Organizational design
- ☐ Complex plan

- ☐ Role specialization (knowledge, skills, and abilities)
- ☐ Changing circumstances
- ☐ Results of a strategic plan
- ☐ Coordination
- ☐ Simple plan

## Analysis

_____

_____

_____

_____

_____

## Personal Reactions

_____

_____

_____

_____

# Mission Impossible (II)*

Color, 1996
Running Time: 1 hour, 50 minutes
Rating: PG-13
Director: Brian DePalma
Distributor: *Paramount Pictures Corporation*

See page 28 for the film description and another scene description.

## Scenes

- **DVD: Chapter 7, Disavowed through Chapter 8, The Black Vault**
- **VHS: (Start: 0:55:42 — Stop: 1:18:27 — 22 minutes)**

These scenes begin as Hunt (Tom Cruise) enters his apartment, takes off his coat, and sits at his laptop computer. They follow the negotiations in the car with Max (Vanessa Redgrave). These scenes end after the operation's completion. The film cuts to a London street scene with the camera panning up the front of an apartment building above the Liverpool Street Underground station (subway station).

## What to Watch for and Ask Yourself

- What are the elements of Hunt's strategic plan? Is it complex or simple? How do they coordinate the plan's elements and team members?
- Does each team member have a specialized role? Do the members have the knowledge, skills, and abilities to carry out their roles?
- Are they prepared for changing circumstances during the operation? Is Hunt aware of the complexity of the operation's environment?

---

*The Roman numeral in parentheses does not refer to the film's version. It denotes the second of two scenes from this version of *Mission Impossible*.

## Concepts or Examples

☐ Strategy

☐ Strategic planning

☐ External environment

☐ Organizational design

☐ Complex plan

☐ Role specialization (knowledge, skills, and abilities

☐ Changing circumstances

☐ Results of a strategic plan

☐ Coordination

☐ Simple plan

## Analysis

_____

_____

_____

_____

_____

## Personal Reactions

_____

_____

_____

_____

# The Secret of My Success (I)

Color, 1987
Running Time: 1 hour, 50 minutes
Rating: PG-13
Director: Herbert Ross
Distributor: *MCA Home Video*

College graduate Brantley Foster (Michael J. Fox) leaves his Kansas home and goes to New York to look for a job. He is continually frustrated in his quest but lands a mailroom job. An entertaining look at corporate life, this film features power, negotiation, and sexual shenanigans. Another film description appears on page 66. Other scene descriptions appear on pages 66 and 68.

## Scenes

- **DVD: Chapter 2, Hired and Fired (Start: 0:05:44 — Stop: 0:07:22)**
- **VHS: (Start: 0:06:32 — Stop: 0:08:11 — 3 minutes)**

These scenes appear early in the film following Brantley's layoff from a job he never started. He looks up at a building saying, "OK New York. If that's the way you want it. OK." They end after Ms. Miller (uncredited) says to Brantley, "Can you be a minority woman?" The film cuts to Brantley talking to his mother on a public telephone.

## What to Watch for and Ask Yourself

- What do these scenes suggest about equal employment opportunity?
- Should Brantley feel that Ms. Miller discriminated against him?
- Assess the actions of the two selection interviewers. Did they behave legally in all respects?

## Concepts or Examples

☐ Job seeking     ☐ Illegal discrimination

☐ Ethical behavior     ☐ Unethical behavior

☐ Equal employment opportunity     ☐ Protected class

☐ Selection interview     ☐ Selection interviewer

## Analysis

_____

_____

_____

_____

_____

## Personal Reactions

_____

_____

_____

_____

_____

# Boycott

Color, 2001
Running Time: 1 hour, 53 minutes
Rating: PG
Director: Clark Johnson
Distributor: *HBO Home Video*

This superbly acted film movingly recreates the early days of the civil rights movement in the United States. The film begins with Rosa Parks' (Iris Little-Thomas) historical moment of not giving her seat to a white man on a segregated Montgomery, Alabama bus. Her single act sparks a successful boycott of the bus system by Montgomery blacks. Jeffrey Wright plays a charismatic Dr. Martin Luther King, Jr., showing the strong leadership he brought to the civil rights movement.

### Scenes
- **DVD: Chapter 1, Introduction/The Ride**
- **VHS: (Start: 0:02:06 — Stop: 0:06:36 — 5 minutes)**

These scenes begin the film after the HBO Films logo. A black title screen gives the date and background of Rosa Parks first bus protest. These scenes end after Rosa Parks' (Iris Little-Thomas) bus sit-in. The bus drives away while Rosa stands in the street looking at the departing bus. The film fades to person writing, "In 1619 the first Negro ..."

### What to Watch for and Ask Yourself
- Do you believe Rosa Parks acted within her rights by not giving her seat to the standing white passenger? Why or why not?
- Note your overall reaction to these scenes. What were your feelings and reactions while watching them?
- How is this moment in American history related to equal employment opportunity and affirmative action today.?

## Concepts or Examples

☐ Basis of civil rights movement

☐ Discrimination

☐ Background to equal em-
ployment opportunity

☐ Racial segregation

☐ Background to affirmative
action

☐ Civil rights

## Analysis

_____

_____

_____

_____

_____

_____

## Personal Reactions

_____

_____

_____

_____

_____

# Legally Blonde

Color, 2001
Running Time: 1 hour, 36 minutes
Rating: PG-13
Director: Robert Luketic
Distributor: *MGM/UA Home Video*

Elle Woods' (Reese Witherspoon) boyfriend, Warner Huntington III (Matthew Davis) wants to go to Harvard Law School instead of keeping their relationship alive. Elle pursues him vigorously by applying to and getting accepted to Harvard Law School. A charming comedy, dedicated to blonde women everywhere in the world. This film is filled with stereotyping, giving it many delightful twists to its surprise conclusion.

## Scenes

- **DVD: Chapter 26, Poor Judgment**
- **VHS: (Start: 1:20:33 — Stop: 1:23:21— 3 minutes)**

These scenes follow the successful use of Elle's hunch about key witness Enrique Salvatore (Greg Serano) in Brooke Windam's (Ali Larter) trial. She enters the law offices area and learns that Professor Callahan (Victor Garber) wants to see her in his office. These scenes end in the elevator as Elle holds her forehead. The film cuts to Elle leaving the elevator in the lobby where she meets Emmett (Luke Wilson) and tells him she is quitting the internship.

## What to Watch for and Ask Yourself

- Does Professor Callahan sexually harass Elle? What is the evidence in these scenes?.
- If these scenes show sexual harassment, what type of harassment is it? Quid pro quo harassment or hostile environment harassment?
- Did Elle behave appropriately or inappropriately in Professor Callahan's office?

## Concepts or Examples

☐ Sexual harassment

☐ Hostile environment harassment

☐ Quid pro quo harassment

☐ Consensual relationship

☐ Different-sex sexual harassment

☐ Same-sex sexual harassment

☐ Supervisor-subordinate relationship

## Analysis

_____

_____

_____

_____

_____

## Personal Reactions

_____

_____

_____

_____

_____

# Wall Street

Color, 1987
Running Time: 2 hours, 4 minutes
Rating: R
Director: Oliver Stone
Distributor: *20th Century Fox Home Entertainment*

Buddy Fox (Charlie Sheen), a young ambitious stock broker wants to learn from the financial wizardry of appropriately reptilian-named Gordan Gekko (Michael Douglas). Buddy does not know the extent of Gekko's unethical behavior to close a deal. Fellow broker Marvin (John C. McGinley) remarks shortly after the selected scenes that Gekko had an ethical bypass at birth. Buddy's eventual discovery of Gekko's evil brings this Oliver Stone film to its predictable end.

## Scenes

- **DVD: Chapter 1, Main Titles (Start: 0:02:37) to Chapter 2, Let's Go to Work! (Stop: 0:06:03)**
- **VHS: (Start: 0:04:54 — Stop: 0:08:15 — 4 minutes)**

These scenes follow the opening shots of Buddy Fox going to work at Jackson-Steinem Co. They begin as the elevator doors open. Buddy and other workers leave the elevator. Carolyn (Tamara Tukie) the receptionist greets him. They end with the shot of the digital clock showing 03:50:22. The film continues with the broker's workday.

## What to Watch for and Ask Yourself

- What is the content of Buddy Fox's job? What knowledge, skills, and abilities (KSAs) does his job require?
- Assess the job context. What working conditions does his job require?
- What are the tasks, duties, and responsibilities of Buddy Fox's job?

## Concepts or Examples

☐ Job content

☐ Knowledge, skills, abilities (KSAs)

☐ Tasks

☐ Job context

☐ Supervision received

☐ Duties

☐ Responsibilities

☐ Equipment used

## Analysis

_____

_____

_____

_____

_____

## Personal Reactions

_____

_____

_____

_____

# Modern Times

Black and White, 1936
Running Time: 1 hour, 27 minutes
Rating: G
Director: Charlie Chaplin
Distributor: *CBS Fox Video*

Charlie Chaplin produced and directed this film and wrote its script and music. It is the last film he made with his Little Tramp character and his first with sound (Maltin 2002, 923; Nowell-Smith 1996, 84–85). It is an engaging satirical portrayal of factory work of the period. The feeding machine sequence early in the film is one of many comic highlights that one should not miss. *Modern Times* ranks among the top 100 films of the American Film Institute and the Library of Congress' National Film Registry (Craddock 2002, 511).

Chaplin plays a factory worker who tightens bolts on nondescript parts that flow endlessly by him. He cracks under the stress of this work and runs crazily through the factory. The entire film features Chaplin trying to rebuild his life around the lovely Paulette Goddard (Chaplin's third wife). They eventually give up in the city and search for a better life elsewhere.

## Scene

- **DVD: Chapter 1, Main Title: The Factory (Start: 0:01:17 — Stop: 0:05:41)**
- **VHS: (Start: 0:05:07 — Stop: 0:09:17 — 4 minutes)**

This scene starts after the opening credits with a close-up shot of a large clock ticking off the time. The text screen reads, "Modern Times. A story of industry, of individual enterprise ~ humanity crusading in the pursuit of happiness." It ends after Chaplin takes his work break. He leaves the work area, punches his time card, goes into the bathroom, and lights a cigarette.

## What to Watch for and Ask Yourself

- On a seven-point scale, assess each job characteristic in the job characteristics model using a scale ranging from a low of 1 to a high of 7.
- Does the job characteristics model predict the level of job satisfaction shown by the workers in the scenes? If *yes*, why?
- How would you redesign these jobs using job enlargement, job rotation, or job enrichment?

## Concepts or Examples

☐ Job design

☐ Job performance

☐ Job satisfaction

☐ Job characteristics: skill variety, autonomy, feedback ...

☐ Co-workers

☐ Job characteristics model

☐ Motivation

☐ Satisfaction

## Analysis

_____

_____

_____

_____

_____

## Personal Reactions

_____

_____

_____

_____

# The Hudsucker Proxy (I)

Color, 1994
Running Time: 1 hour, 51 minutes
Rating: PG
Director: Joel Coen
Distributor: *Warner Home Video*

Norville Barnes (Tim Robbins), a graduate of the Muncie College of Business Administration, quickly moves from mailroom clerk to President of Hudsucker Industries. The board of directors appoints him in the hope that his incompetence will drive down the stock price so they can buy a controlling interest. Norville has his own idea for a product, a simple plastic hoop. After a slow start in sales, the hula-hoop becomes a success, drives the stock price up, and causes the board great distress. Sidney J. Mussburger (Paul Newman) aspires to the presidency and sabotages Norville by presenting him as insane. The film takes a delightful twist at the end when Norville inherits the late Waring Hudsucker's fortune, regains the presidency, and presents the board with a new product idea—the Frisbee. *The Hudsucker Proxy* is the first major mainstream effort of the maverick Coen brothers. Other film and scene descriptions appear on page 54.

## Scenes

- **DVD: Chapter 23, Norville's dingus to Chapter 25, Jumping through hoops (Stop: 1:04:47)**
- **VHS: (Start: 1:03:17 — Stop: 1:08:03 — 5 minutes)**

The scenes start with a woman saying "Shh!" to the camera. It zooms to a sign on the boardroom door that reads, "Quiet Please! Board Meeting in Session." These scenes follow Norville's romantic evening with Amy Archer (Jennifer Jason Leigh). They end after the hula-hoop sign appears in the window of a toy store and the store owner steps outside. The film cuts to Norville Barnes' office and Amy looking at a ticker tape.

## What to Watch for and Ask Yourself

- Which types of organizational design do these scenes show?
- Which organizational design characteristics appear in these scenes?
- Do these scenes show any behavioral demands of organizational design? What are they?

## Concepts or Examples

☐ Organizational design by division

☐ Organizational design by function

☐ Hybrid organizational design

☐ Matrix organizational design

☐ Self-managing teams

☐ Process view of organizational design

☐ Simple, static environment

☐ Complex, dynamic environment

## Analysis

_____

_____

_____

_____

_____

_____

## Personal Reactions

_____

_____

_____

_____

# The Firm (I)

Color, 1993
Running Time: 2 hours, 34 minutes
Rating: R
Director: Sidney Pollack
Distributor: *Paramount Pictures Corporation*

Mitch McDeere (Tom Cruise) graduates from Harvard Law School with honors and in the top five of his class. Many top law firms vigorously recruit him. Mitch chooses a small Memphis, Tennessee firm with a large starting salary, a new Mercedes, and a low-interest home mortgage. He quickly learns that "The Firm" is entangled in a web of murder and corruption.* See page 46 for a description of another scene from this film.

## Scenes

- **DVD: Chapter 1, Opening Credits (Start: 0:00:18) to Chapter 2, We Want You (Stop: 0:07:24)**
- **VHS: (Start: 0:04:52 — Stop: 0:11:58 — 7 minutes)**

Two sets of scenes show different parts of the recruiting process. This first set shows the on-campus recruiting efforts. The second set [*The Firm* (II), pages 46–47] shows Mitch and his wife Abby's (Jeanne Tripplehorn) visit to the firm in Memphis, Tennessee.

This sequence begins the film after the Paramount logo and a black screen. It includes the opening credits. This sequence ends after Abby's comment about why did Mitch get such an offer and they kiss. The film cuts to an aerial panning shot of Memphis.

## What to Watch for and Ask Yourself

- What expectations does Mitch develop about the firm during his campus interview?
- Are his expectations realistic about working for the firm. (**Note:** If you have seen this film, try to ignore your knowledge of later developments.)
- Assess all aspects of the firm's recruitment process while on the Harvard University campus. Did they behave ethically or unethically, legally or illegally?

---

*Film and scene descriptions adapted from J. E. Champoux, Seeing and Valuing Diversity Through Film, *Educational Media International* 36 (December 1999): 310–316. © Taylor & Francis Ltd., P. O. Box 25, Abingdon, Oxfordshire, OX14 3UE. Reprinted by permission.

## Concepts or Examples

☐ Recruitment process
☐ Campus recruitment
☐ Company recruiters
☐ Internal recruiting

☐ Expectations
☐ Ethical behavior
☐ Unethical behavior
☐ External recruiting

## Analysis

_____

_____

_____

_____

_____

## Personal Reactions

_____

_____

_____

_____

# The Firm (II)

Color, 1993
Running Time: 2 hours, 34 minutes
Rating: R
Director: Sidney Pollack
Distributor: *Paramount Pictures Corporation*

See page 44 for the film description and another scene description.

## Scenes

- **DVD: Chapter 2, We Want You (Start: 0:07:25) to Chapter 3, The Family (Stop: 0:12:19)**
- **VHS: (Start: 0:11:59 — Stop: 0:16:55 — 5 minutes)**

The second set of scenes starts right after the first set. They begin with an aerial panning shot of Memphis. The sequence ends as Mitch (Tom Cruise) and his wife Abby (Jeanne Tripplehorn) embrace following their discussion about accepting the firm's offer. The film cuts to Oliver Lambert's (Hal Holbrook) office and a discussion about Abby's telephone calls while in Memphis.[*]

## What to Watch for and Ask Yourself

- What expectations does Mitch develop about the firm during the Memphis visit?
- What expectations does Abby develop during their Memphis visit? Should she share them more fully with Mitch?
- Does Mitch now have a realistic image of what it will be like to work for the firm?

---

[*]Scene description adapted from J. E. Champoux, Seeing and Valuing Diversity Through Film, *Educational Media International* 36 (December 1999): 310–316. © Taylor & Francis Ltd., P. O. Box 25, Abingdon, Oxfordshire, OX14 3UE. Reprinted by permission.

## Concepts or Examples

☐ Recruitment process                    ☐ External recruiting

☐ Internal recruiting                    ☐ On-site recruiting visit

☐ Expectations

## Analysis

_____

_____

_____

_____

_____

## Personal Reactions

_____

_____

_____

_____

# Crimson Tide

Color, 1995
Running Time: 1 hour, 56 minutes
Rating: R
Director: Tony Scott
Distributor: *Hollywood Pictures Home Video*

*T*he *Caine Mutiny* meets *The Hunt for Red October* in this post-cold war military drama. The *U.S.S. Alabama*, a nuclear submarine, has set to sea with new Executive Officer (XO) Lt. Commander Ron Hunter (Denzel Washington). Events in Russia push that country and the United States to the brink of war. This tense situation causes Captain Ramsey (Gene Hackman) to become too mentally unstable to make the fateful decision to launch the *Alabama's* nuclear missiles.

## Scene

- **DVD: Chapter 2, Welcome Aboard**
- **VHS: (Start: 0:09:53 — Stop: 0:12:05 — 2 minutes)**

This scene starts at the end of the opening credits. It begins with a shot of Captain Ramsey's dog Bear lying on a pillow and the title screen, "Directed by Tony Scott." The scene ends after Ramsey says, "Welcome aboard the Alabama, son. Do me proud." Chief of the Boat (COB, George Dzundza) says, "Welcome aboard Mr. Hunter." The film cuts to a television newscast some officers are watching in the briefing room. (This scene has one instance of R-rated language.)

## What to Watch for and Ask Yourself

- What job-related selection criteria does Captain Ramsey use to choose Lt. Commander Hunter?
- Does he use any non-job-related selection criteria?
- Do you expect Hunter to perform as expected? Why or why not?

## Concepts or Examples

☐ Selection process

☐ Job-related selection criteria

☐ Selection and performance

☐ Selection criteria validity

☐ Background check

☐ Behavioral observations

☐ Selection tests

☐ Nonjob-related selection criteria

## Analysis

_____

_____

_____

_____

_____

## Personal Reactions

_____

_____

_____

_____

# Bowfinger (I)

Color, 1999
Running Time: 1 hour, 37 minutes
Rating: PG-13
Director: Frank Oz
Distributor: *Universal Home Video*

This first-time combination of Steve Martin and Eddie Murphy offers a funny look at a twist on Hollywood film making. Bobby Bowfinger (Martin), perhaps film makings least successful director, wants to produce a low-budget film with top star Kit Ramsey (Murphy). Bowfinger's problem: recruit a crew and cast with almost no budget and trick Kit into appearing in his film. See page 52 for a description of another scene from this film.

## Scenes

- **DVD: Chapter 11, The Lookalike**
- **VHS: (Start: 0:57:00 — Stop: 1:00:09 — 3 minutes)**

These scenes start with a close-up of Bobbie Bowfinger (Steve Martin) counting money at his desk. Dave (Jamie Kennedy) enters Bobbie's office saying he cannot find Kit. The scenes follow Kit's stress reactions and discussion with his doctor about going to a relaxation center. These scenes end after Jiffernson (Jiff) Ramsey (Eddie Murphy), Kit's brother, receives his wardrobe. The film cuts to a shot of a busy Los Angeles freeway.

## What to Watch for and Ask Yourself

- Does Bobbie Bowfinger have a set of valid selection criteria to fill the role of a Kit Ramsey lookalike? Does Bowfinger apply the criteria uniformly to each role applicant?
- Is there a good person-job fit of Jiff Ramsey in the screen role of Kit Ramsey?
- Do you predict Jiff Ramsey's success as a Kit Ramsey substitute?

## Concepts or Examples

☐ Selection process

☐ Selection criteria

☐ Selection criteria validity

☐ Uniform application of selection criteria

☐ Job placement

☐ Person-job fit

## Analysis

_____

_____

_____

_____

_____

## Personal Reactions

_____

_____

_____

_____

# Bowfinger (II)

Color, 1999
Running Time: 1 hour, 37 minutes
Rating: PG-13
Director: Frank Oz
Distributor: *Universal Home Video*

See page 50 for the film description and another scene description.

## Scene

- **DVD: Chapter 12, The Freeway Scene (Stop: 0:52:50)**
- **VHS: (Start: 1:00:10 — Stop: 1:03:39 — 4 minutes)**

This scene immediately follows the scenes of recruiting a Kit Ramsey lookalike. It starts with a shot of a busy Los Angeles freeway. This scene ends after everyone congratulates Kit (Eddie Murphy) on his excellent performance and Bowfinger (Steve Martin) asks him to repeat the scene. The film cuts to the crew unloading the van at Bowfinger's house.

## What to Watch for and Ask Yourself

- Is there a good person-job fit for Kit Ramsey?
- Were Bobbie Bowfinger's selection criteria valid for the job of running errands?
- Assess Kit's first workday job performance. Did he perform as expected?

## Concepts or Examples

☐ Person-job fit                              ☐ On-the-job performance

☐ Selection and placement                     ☐ Valid selection criteria

☐ Invalid selection criteria

## Analysis

_____

_____

_____

_____

_____

## Personal Reactions

_____

_____

_____

_____

---

# The Hudsucker Proxy (II)

Color, 1994
Running Time: 1 hour, 51 minutes
Rating: PG
Director: Joel Coen
Distributor: *Warner Home Video*

This is another look at Norville Barnes (Tim Robbins), the mailroom clerk who unexpectedly becomes president of Hudsucker Industries. He also invents the hula-hoop and the Frisbee. For a more detailed film description and another scene description, see page 42.

## Scenes

- **DVD: Chapter 5, Mailroom orientation to Chapter 6, Norville's ticket upstairs (Stop: 0:17:42)**
- **VHS: (Start: 0:16:35 — Stop: 0:21:14 — 5 minutes)**

These scenes start as Norville enters the mailroom pushing his mail basket and listening to directions from his mailroom orienter (Christopher Darga). They follow Sidney J. Mussburger's (Paul Newman) presentation to the board of his idea to appoint an idiot as president. These scenes end after Norville receives the Blue Letter to deliver. The film cuts to an opening elevator door.

## What to Watch for and Ask Yourself

- Critique Norville's orientation. What does he learn about Hudsucker Industries, the mail room, co-workers, and supervision?
- What are the sources of Norville's socialization experiences? Do these experiences improve his person-organization fit with Hudsucker Industries? Why or why not?
- Does he learn any critical role behaviors during his first workday orientation?

## Concepts or Examples

- ☐ Orientation and socialization
- ☐ Person-organization fit
- ☐ Sources of socialization (supervisor, co-workers)
- ☐ Motivation to learn

- ☐ Critical role behaviors
- ☐ Learn about co-workers
- ☐ Learn about supervision
- ☐ Learn about Hudsucker Industries

## Analysis

_____

_____

_____

_____

## Personal Reactions

_____

_____

_____

_____

# The Full Monty

Color, 1997
Running Time: 1 hour, 35 minutes
Rating: R
Director: Peter Cattaneo
Distributor: *Twentieth Century Fox Home Entertainment*

Six unemployed Yorkshire mill workers try to find ways of making money. After noticing that women flocked to a Chippendale's performance, they decide to design their own act. These fellows are not Chippendale's materials. They range from young to middle aged; slender to overweight. There are many laughs in this charming British film that is filled with British slang. The title means they must strip totally naked. *

## Scenes

- **DVD: Chapter 10, Pillow Talk (Start: 0:39:01) to Chapter 11, Dressing Down (Stop: 0:42:18)**
- **VHS: (Start: 0:39:27 — Stop: 0:42:45 — 3 minutes)**

These scenes follow Dave's (Mark Addy) interactions with Gaz (Robert Carlyle) and Gaz's son Nathan (William Snape) in a supermarket. He steals a copy of the film *Flashdance* (1983). The scenes start with images from *Flashdance* playing on a television monitor. They will soon begin their training for their full monty performance. Gerald (Tom Wilkinson) is the instructor because of his dance experience. These scenes end after Gerald stops the music and says, "Perfect." Dave says, "Well, you should have said." The film cuts to an outside shot of Gerald's house. The men arrive for their first meeting where they disrobe in front of each other. (These scenes have some R-rated language.)

## What to Watch for and Ask Yourself

- Are the men motivated to learn? Do they have the ability to learn? What is the evidence in the scenes?
- Are there moments of behavior modeling? If *yes*, by whom?
- Does Gerald as the trainer shape behavior by reinforcement and immediate confirmation? How?

---

*Film description adapted from J. E. Champoux, Seeing and Valuing Diversity Through Film, *Educational Media International* 36 (December 1999): 310–316. © Taylor & Francis Ltd., P. O. Box 25, Abingdon, Oxfordshire, OX14 3UE. Reprinted by permission.

## Concepts or Examples

☐ Ability to learn         ☐ Shaping behavior (reinforcement, immediate confirmation

☐ Experience (Horse)

☐ Behavior modeling         ☐ Training readiness

☐ Self-efficacy         ☐ Motivation to learn

## Analysis

_____

_____

_____

_____

_____

## Personal Reactions

_____

_____

_____

# Up Close & Personal (I)

Color, 1996
Running Time: 2 hours, 4 minutes
Rating: PG-13
Director: John Avnet
Distributor: *Touchstone Home Video*

Ambitious Sally (Tally)[*] Atwater (Michelle Pfeiffer) wants to break into television news reporting. She gets her chance when veteran television news reporter Warren Justice (Robert Redford) hires her at a Miami station. Romance follows, making their relationship complex and at times tumultuous. This well-acted film, based on a screenplay by novelists Joan Didion and John Gregory Dunne, has much comedy—and a sad ending.[†] See page 60 for another scene description from this film.

## Scenes

- **DVD Chapter 2, the newsroom (Start: 0:11:02) to Chapter 3, tally's debut (Stop: 0:16:36)**
- **VHS (Start: 0:14:04 — Stop: 0:19:38 — 6 minutes)**

These scenes start with a close-up of Warren's laundry that Sally picked up for him. They begin after her first day on the job. The scenes end after Sally jerks off the raincoat and leaves the studio. Warren goes down the stairs. The film cuts to a night shot of him arriving at Sally's apartment building in his car.[‡]

## What to Watch for and Ask Yourself

- Do these scenes show only training or do they include employee development? What is Warren Justice's role in Sally's training?
- Does Sally's performance improve because of the training? If *yes*, in what specific ways?
- Is Sally a good choice, and a good fit, for the weather reporter role? Do you think she would perform better in another role? Why or why not?

---

[*]Her on-air name changes to Tally during her first on-camera effort as the weather forecaster.

[†]Film and scene descriptions adapted from J. E. Champoux, Seeing and Valuing Diversity Through Film, *Educational Media International* 36 (December 1999): 310–316. © Taylor & Francis Ltd., P. O. Box 25, Abingdon, Oxfordshire, OX14 3UE. Reprinted by permission.

[‡]Professor Beth Crockford, Colby-Sawyer College, first recommended scenes from this film to me, September 21, 2000—J.E.C.

## Concepts or Examples

☐ Training                    ☐ Mentoring / coaching

☐ Job performance             ☐ Job-site development

☐ Performance improvement     ☐ Employee development

## Analysis

_____

_____

_____

_____

## Personal Reactions

_____

_____

_____

_____

_____

# Up Close & Personal (II)

Color, 1996
Running Time: 2 hours, 4 minutes
Rating: PG-13
Director: John Avnet
Distributor: *Touchstone Home Video*

See page 58 for the film description and a description of another scene from *Up Close & Personal.*

## Scenes

- **DVD Chapter 4, promotion (Start: 0:18:41 — Stop: 0:24:34)**
- **VHS (Start: 0:21:45 — Stop: 0:27:36 — 6 minutes)**

These scenes begin as the camera pans across the Channel 9 news assignment board. They follow Warren Justice's (Robert Redford) visit to Sally Atwater's (Michelle Pfeiffer) apartment telling her he promoted her to reporter. It ends after Warren gives Sally a bottle of water. The film cuts to an outside panning shot of the Channel 9 news building.

## What to Watch for and Ask Yourself

- Do these scenes show training or employee development? What is Warren Justice's role in Sally's training and development?
- Does Sally's performance improve as a result of the development effort? If *yes*, in what specific ways?
- Is Sally a good choice, and a better fit, to the news reporter role than the weather reporter role? Why or why not?

## Concepts or Examples

☐ Training                  ☐ Mentoring / coaching

☐ Job performance           ☐ Job-site development

☐ Employee development      ☐ Performance improvement

## Analysis

_____

_____

_____

_____

_____

## Personal Reactions

_____

_____

_____

_____

# Dirty Dancing (I)

Color, 1987
Running Time: 1 hour, 55 minutes
Rating: PG-13
Director: Emile Arolino
Distributor: *Vestron Video*

I f you like 1960s rock-and-roll music and dancing, you will enjoy this film. Innocent, young Baby Houseman (Jennifer Grey) vacations in the Catskill mountains with her parents. Bored with the scheduled activities, she eventually becomes involved with handsome dance instructor Johnny Castle (Patrick Swayze). See page 64 for a description of another scene from this film.

### Scenes

- **DVD: Chapter 18, Hungry Eyes (Start: 0:36:11) through Chapter 20, Hey Baby**
- **VHS: (Start: 0:35:28 — Stop: 0:44:02 — 9 minutes)**

These scenes start with Baby running up to the dance studio building as "Hungry Eyes" plays in the background. They follow her earlier dance lessons with Johnny. Baby must learn the lift, her most difficult dance move. These scenes end with Johnny and Baby in the lake, successfully finishing the lift. The film cuts to Penny (Cynthia Rhodes) and Baby walking toward a lodge building.

### What to Watch for and Ask Yourself

- Think of Johnny Castle as a manager in his relationship to Baby. Does he set clear performance standards and identify performance requirements?
- Does he encourage Baby to improve her dance performance? If *yes*, how?
- How does he measure her performance and give Baby performance feedback?

## Concepts or Examples

☐ Identify performance requirements

☐ Performance rewards

☐ Coaching

☐ Encourage performance

☐ Improve performance

☐ Measure performance

☐ Performance standards

## Analysis

_____

_____

_____

_____

_____

## Personal Reactions

_____

_____

_____

_____

# Dirty Dancing (II)

Color, 1987
Running Time: 1 hour, 55 minutes
Rating: PG-13
Director: Emile Arolino
Distributor: *Vestron Video*

See page 62 for the film description and another scene description.

## Scenes

- **DVD: Chapter 42, "Nobody Puts Baby in a Corner" (Start: 1:28:42) to Chapter 43, (I've Had) The Time of My Life (Stop: 1:33:42)**
- **VHS: (Start: 1:29:58 — Stop: 1:34:59 — 5 minutes)**

These scenes start as Johnny Castle (Patrick Swayze) enters the Sheldrake Lodge. They follow the opening of the lodge's last night and a close-up of Baby Houseman (Jennifer Grey) listening to the singers on stage. These scenes end as Baby finishes her lift and she and Johnny embrace. The film continues with the excited audience's involvement in the dance.

## What to Watch for and Ask Yourself

- Do Johnny's performance management efforts get the desired results?
- Does Baby show performance improvement and development compared to her performance in the first set of scenes?
- Does Baby receive any rewards for performance improvement and development? If *yes*, what are they?

## Concepts or Examples

- ☐ Performance management
- ☐ Performance development
- ☐ Failure to meet performance goals

- ☐ Performance improvement
- ☐ Meeting performance goals
- ☐ Performance rewards

## Analysis

_____

_____

_____

_____

_____

## Personal Reactions

_____

_____

_____

_____

# The Secret of My Success (IIa)

Color, 1987
Running Time: 1 hour, 50 minutes
Rating: PG-13
Director: Herbert Ross
Distributor: *MCA Home Video*

An entertaining look at corporate life, this film features negotiation, power, and sexual shenanigans. A more detailed description of this film appears on page 32. See pages 32 and 68 for descriptions of other scenes from *The Secret of My Success*.

## Scenes

- **DVD: Chapter 15, The Party (Start: 1:25:57 — Stop: 1:27:51)**
- **VHS: (Start: 1:26:36 — Stop: 1:28:42 — 2 minutes)**

These scenes start at Howard Prescott's (Richard Jordan) garden party shortly after Brantley (Michael J. Fox) and Christy Wills (Helen Slater) have a liaison in the bushes. Brantley is now Carlton Whitfield, a knowledgeable staff member. The scenes begin as Prescott discusses a report with his staff. They end as Vera Prescott (Margaret Whitton) smiles. The film cuts to Howard Prescott walking across the lawn, searching for Christy.

## What to Watch for and Ask Yourself

- What do these scenes suggest about career management and career transition?
- Do the scenes show Brantley (Carlton) forming alliances? Can such networks and alliances help one move ahead in a career? Why?
- Critique Brantley's self-presentation. How well does he interact and present himself to the business people to whom Vera Prescott has introduced him?

## Concepts or Examples

☐ Self-presentation

☐ Impression management

☐ Networking and alliances

☐ Pursue personal interests

☐ Career transition

☐ Individual-centered career management

☐ Organization-centered career management

☐ Career planning

## Analysis

_____

_____

_____

_____

_____

## Personal Reactions

_____

_____

_____

_____

# The Secret of My Success (IIb)

Color, 1987
Running Time: 1 hour, 50 minutes
Rating: PG-13
Director: Herbert Ross
Distributor: *MCA Home Video*

See page 32 for a detailed film description. Pages 32 and 66 have other scene descriptions.

## Scenes

- **DVD: Chapter 18, Outdoing Mr. Davenport**
  **(Start: 1:39:51 — Stop: 1:44:31)**
- **VHS: (Start: 1:40:30 — Stop: 1:45:12 — 5 minutes)**

This scene follows Brantley (Michael J. Fox), Christy (Helen Slater), and others preparing to leave the company. Brantley and Christy return to his former office to begin working on his new idea. The scene opens with a board and staff meeting discussing the merger proposal from Davenport Industries. Howard Prescott (Richard Jordan) begins the discussions. The scene ends after Brantley hugs Melrose (John Pankow). The film cuts to elevator doors opening and Brantley and Christy getting into the elevator.

## What to Watch for and Ask Yourself

- Did the alliances Brantley formed in the first set of scenes [*The Secret of My Success* (IIa), pages 66–67] help him in this last step of his career management?
- Did he behave ethically or unethically?
- Assess Brantley's behavior in these scenes. Could such behavior create problems for a person trying to advance his or her career?

## Concepts or Examples

☐ Career management        ☐ Ethical behavior

☐ Alliances and networks      ☐ Unethical behavior

☐ Risk taking behavior

## Analysis

_____

_____

_____

_____

_____

## Personal Reactions

_____

_____

_____

_____

_____

# Jerry Maguire

Color, 1996
Running Time: 2 hours, 15 minutes
Rating: R
Director: Cameron Crowe
Distributor: *Columbia Tristar Home Video*

Did the now well-remembered line, "Show me the money!" help win Cuba Gooding a Best Supporting Actor Oscar? Likely Gooding's performance as obnoxious football player Rod Tidwell helped. This lengthy story about sports, athletes, and sports agents follows Jerry Maguire (Tom Cruise) after he gains a conscience about representing athletes. His moral awakening leads to his termination and tenacious hold on one remaining client—Tidwell. See Peske and West (1999, 14) for a humorous female view of this film.

## Scenes

- **DVD: Chapter 5, Fired to Chapter 7, Coming with him (Stop: 0:32:51)**
- **VHS: (Start: 0:25:20 — Stop: 0:37:37 — 12 minutes)**

This sequence starts with Jerry Maguire arriving at Cronin's Restaurant for a luncheon meeting with Bob Sugar (Jay Mohr). The sequence ends with a wide, almost aerial shot of the work area as the employees return to normal work activities. The film cuts to Dorothy Boyd (Renée Zellweger) and Jerry on the elevator with the goldfish in a bag. (These scenes have some R-rated language.)*

## What to Watch for and Ask Yourself

- Assess Bob Sugar's method of discharging Jerry Maguire.
- Did he behave ethically or unethically? Include his behavior after ending Jerry's employment.
- Can employment terminations affect co-workers in positive and negative ways?

*First recommended to me by Lou Ann Branch, MBA student, Robert O. Anderson Graduate School of Management, University of New Mexico, May 12, 1998. – J.E.C.

## Concepts or Examples

- ☐ Separation and retention
- ☐ Emotional effects
- ☐ Effects on co-workers
- ☐ Employee loyalty

- ☐ Discharge interview
- ☐ Ethical behavior
- ☐ Unethical behavior
- ☐ Employee discharge

## Analysis

_____

_____

_____

_____

_____

## Personal Reactions

_____

_____

_____

_____

_____

---

# Mr. Holland's Opus

Color, 1995
Running Time: 2 hours, 22 minutes
Rating: PG
Director: Stephen Herek
Distributor: *Buena Vista Home Video*

Glenn Holland (Richard Dreyfuss) has an undying passion for music but must leave full-time composing to accept a high school music teacher's job. Originally intended as a temporary position, Holland stays for thirty years. During that time, he discovers his gifts as a teacher and his ability to motivate his students to high performance.

## Scenes

- **DVD: Chapter 10, New Assignment (Start 0:45:47) to Chapter 11, Challenged (Stop: 0:53:51)**
- **VHS: (Start: 0:51:10 — Stop: 0:59:13 — 8 minutes)**

This sequence starts on the school's football field after Mr. Holland's unsuccessful effort at getting the band to march correctly. It follows Mr. Holland's discussion with Principal Jacobs (Olympia Dukakis) and Vice Principal Wolters (William H. Macy) about the type of music he teaches. They appointed him the head of the marching band.

Mr. Holland has great difficulty getting the band to march correctly. Coach Meister (Jay Thomas) intervenes. A little later he says to Mr. Holland, "You see this kid up in the stands here. It's Lou Russ." The sequence ends after Mr. Holland and the band congratulate Lou (Terrence Howard) for getting the beat. The film cuts to the town's parade.

## What to Watch for and Ask Yourself

- What motivational method does Mr. Holland use to motivate Lou Russ to learn to play the drum?
- Does he change Lou's playing behavior gradually or in one large change?
- What happens to Lou's self-esteem as these scenes unfold?

## Concepts or Examples

☐ Motivation           ☐ Positive reinforcement

☐ Behavior modification     ☐ Self-esteem

☐ Shaping               ☐ Esteem needs

## Analysis

_____

_____

_____

_____

_____

## Personal Reactions

_____

_____

_____

_____

_____

---

# Tootsie

Color, 1982
Running Time: 1 hour, 51 minutes
Rating: PG
Director: Sydney Pollack
Distributor: *RCA/Columbia Pictures Home Video*

Michael Dorsey (Dustin Hoffman) has alienated every New York producer. Failing to get a job as a man, he changes his identity to a woman—Dorothy Michaels. Dorothy quickly lands a soap opera role where she becomes highly popular. Along the way, Michael falls in love with his (her!) co-star Julie (Jessica Lange) while Julie's father Les (Charles Durning) falls in love with Dorothy. Director Sydney Pollack plays Michael's agent George Fields. The American Film Institute ranks *Tootsie* in its top 100 films (Craddock 2002, 772).

## Scene
- **DVD: Chapter 25, Late-Night Visit (Stop: 1:38:45)**
- **VHS: (Start: 1:37:53 — Stop: 1:39:18 — 2 minutes**

This scene begins with George (Sydney Pollack) pouring a drink while saying, "It's two o'clock in the morning, Michael. Can't this wait?" It follows Michael's hostile interaction with Sandy (Teri Garr) in his apartment. The scene ends after Michael says, "I'm in trouble man." The film cuts to the control room where Ron Carlisle (Dabney Coleman) directs a segment of the show.

The following are important contextual facts for understanding this scene.

- Les wants to marry Dorothy.
- Julie thinks Dorothy is gay.
- Dorothy (Michael) is straight.
- Michael is falling for Julie.
- Sandy thinks Michael is gay.

## What to Watch for and Ask Yourself

- Does noise and distortion surround this communication process? If *yes*, what is the source?
- Does Michael clearly describe various people's perceptions of Michael and Dorothy?
- At the end of the process, does George completely understand what Michael said?

## Concepts or Examples

☐ Communication

☐ Miscommunication

☐ Frame of reference

☐ Noise in the communication process

☐ Communication dysfunction

☐ Listening

## Analysis

_____

_____

_____

_____

_____

_____

## Personal Reactions

_____

_____

_____

_____

_____

# Boiler Room

Color, 2000
Running Time: 2 hours
Rating: R
Director: Ben Younger
Distributor: *New Line Home Video*

Young Seth (Giovanni Ribisi) joins J.T. Marlin, a brokerage firm, where he hopes to become rich. Seth works with other young, eager people in the "Boiler Room," a call center for contacting prospective clients. High-pressure selling tactics raise many ethical issues for Seth, although other traders easily brush away the dilemmas. He begins to suspect the firm's method of trading stocks. Seth eventually discovers that the firm is under investigation for illegal trading.

## Scenes
- **DVD: Chapter 22, "Congratulations!"**
- **VHS: (Start: 1:25:05 — Stop: 1:27:18 — 2 minutes)**

These scenes start with an outside panning shot of the building and a cut to everyone talking in the "Boiler Room." The scenes follow the altercation between Greg (Nicky Katt) and Seth. They end after Michael (Tom Edward Scott) raises his glass at the party while saying, "We're players now, boys! Let's celebrate! Salud!" The film fades to black and cuts to Seth peering in the window of Med Patent Technologies.

## What to Watch for and Ask Yourself
- Does Michael use positive reinforcement? What does he specifically do?
- What incentives does Michael outline for his sales force?
- Is the sales force highly motivated to sell stock shares?

## Concepts or Examples

☐ Motivation    ☐ Rewards

☐ Positive reinforcement  ☐ Incentives

☐ Recognition    ☐ Compensation

## Analysis

_____

_____

_____

_____

_____

## Personal Reactions

_____

_____

_____

_____

_____

---

# 9 to 5

Color, 1980
Running Time: 1 hour, 50 minutes
Rating: PG
Director: Colin Higgins
Distributor: *Twentieth Century Fox Home Entertainment*

An office manager and two secretaries discover they share the same view of their boss. He is sexist and egocentric. They plot to take over the office and succeed. Their efforts turn the office into a model of smooth operation with satisfied workers.

## Scenes

- **DVD: Chapter 16, Mr. Hart Returns (Start: 1:40:50) to Chapter 17, Brazil (Stop: 1:45:25)**
- **VHS: (Start: 1:43:04 — Stop: 1:47:41 — 5 minutes)**

These scenes start with company board chair Mr. Russell Tinsworthy (Sterling Hayden) coming down the hall leading a group of managers. The sound of snare drums introduces Mr. Tinsworthy. The group approaches Franklin Hart (Dabney Coleman). Mr. Hinkle (Henry Jones) says, "Here's the man himself, Mr. Tinsworthy. Franklin Hart." These scenes follow Hart's frantic, stressed preparation in his office with Violet (Lily Tomlin) for meeting Tinsworthy. These scenes end as the elevator doors close with Hart saying, "Brazil?" The film cuts to a close-up of Doralee (Dolly Parton) opening a bottle of champagne.

## What to Watch for and Ask Yourself

- How many employee benefits can you identify in these scenes?
- Do these benefits exist today?
- What effect can such benefits have on employees? Do they motivate higher job performance or improve employee retention?

## Concepts or Examples

☐ Personal needs

☐ Job sharing program

☐ Day care center

☐ Policy effects

☐ Employee motivation

☐ Alcoholic rehabilitation center

☐ Human resource management policies

☐ Employee retention

## Analysis

_____

_____

_____

_____

_____

_____

## Personal Reactions

_____

_____

_____

_____

_____

# The Paper

Color, 1994
Running Time: 1 hour, 52 minutes
Rating: R
Director: Ron Howard
Distributor: *MCA Universal Home Video*

This engaging film shows the ethical dilemmas and stress of producing a daily newspaper, *The New York Sun*. Editor Henry Hackett (Michael Keaton) races against the clock to produce a story that describes a major police scandal that could send two young black men to jail. He is in constant conflict with his managing editor, Alicia Clark (Glenn Close), whose ambitions focus her more on budget control than running true stories. Hackett also has constant pressure from his wife, Marty (Marisa Tomei), who is pregnant with their first child. She wants him to take a less demanding job and continually pushes for that while Hackett tries to get the story he wants.*

## Scenes

- **DVD Chapter 12, Stop the presses! to Chapter 13, The punchout in the pressroom (Stop: 1:27:35)**
- **VHS (Start: 1:25:36 — Stop: 1:30:24 — 5 minutes)**

These scenes follow Henry Hackett and McDougal (Randy Quaid) discovering that the newspaper is printing the wrong headline. They start with Alicia Clark peering through some office window blinds. She enters the newsroom and finds a reporter preparing a new headline to replace one already on the presses. They end after Henry Hackett says, "Hey Alicia! ... Congratulations. ... You have officially become everything you used to hate." Alicia, Henry, and McDougal leave the pressroom. The original versions of the newspaper continue to come off the presses. The film cuts to an outside shot showing McDougal's car being towed away. (These scenes have R-rated language.)

## What to Watch for and Ask Yourself

- What do these scenes suggest about workplace safety?
- Do these scenes show a realistic situation for today's workplace?
- Should Human Resource management departments offer counseling for employees prone to violent behavior? Why or why not?

---

*Film description adapted from J. E. Champoux, Seeing and Valuing Diversity Through Film, *Educational Media International* 36 (December 1999): 310–316. © Taylor & Francis Ltd., P. O. Box 25, Abingdon, Oxfordshire, OX14 3UE. Reprinted by permission.

## Concepts or Examples

- ☐ Employee discharge
- ☐ Unethical behavior
- ☐ Workplace violence

- ☐ Workplace safety
- ☐ Ethical dilemma
- ☐ Ethical behavior

## Analysis

_____

_____

_____

_____

_____

## Personal Reactions

_____

_____

_____

_____

_____

_____

# Norma Rae (I)

Color, 1979
Running Time: 1 hour, 54 minutes
Rating: PG
Director: Martin Ritt
Distributor: *CBS Fox Video*

This powerful drama shows the struggle of Southern textile workers in forming their first labor union. Reuben (Ron Leibman), a New York City labor organizer, inspires Norma Rae (Sally Field) to organize her fellow workers. Based on true events, Norma Rae's leadership skills get the desired results. Field received a Best Actress Academy Award for her performance. See page 84 for a description of another scene from this film.

## Scenes

- **DVD: Chapter 12, What a Union Is**
- **VHS: Start: 0:46:08 — Stop: 0:56:07 — 10 minutes)**

The scenes begin with a shot of Norma Rae holding a TWUA (Textile Workers Union of America) flyer announcing a union organizing meeting that evening. These scenes follow her wedding. They end as the managers move the stock blocking the bulletin board and the shot of a pensive Norma Rae. The film cuts to Norma Rae crossing a motel parking lot.

## What to Watch for and Ask Yourself

- What motivates these workers to form a union?
- Does management accept the workers' legal right to organize?
- What are the working conditions of these workers?

## Concepts or Examples

☐ Union

☐ Union-management relations

☐ Poor working conditions

☐ Motivation to organize

☐ Oppressive supervision

☐ People as machines

☐ Hostile management

☐ Management interference with organizing effort

☐ Illegal interference

## Analysis

_____

_____

_____

_____

_____

## Personal Reactions

_____

_____

_____

_____

# Norma Rae (II)

Color, 1979
Running Time: 1 hour, 54 minutes
Rating: PG
Director: Martin Ritt
Distributor: *CBS Fox Video*

See page 82 for the film description and a description of another scene from *Norma Rae*.

## Scenes
- **DVD: Chapter 30, Union!**
- **VHS: (Start: 1:47:25 — Stop: 1:51:14 — 4 minutes)**

These scenes appear at the end of the film after Norma Rae (Sally Field) defied management and displayed the "Union" sign. They follow the scene of her husband Sonny (Beau Bridges) reaffirming his love for her. The scenes start with a shot of two workers tallying the union vote ballots. They end with the managers leaving the hall followed by the press as the workers cheer their victory. The film cuts to an outside shot of Reuben (Ron Leibman) and Norma Rae listening to the workers' cheers outside the plant's gate.

## What to Watch for and Ask Yourself
- What is your reaction to the workers' elation at winning the union representation election?
- Are they right or wrong in voting for the union?
- What do you believe was the nature of union-management relations before the vote? Were they good or bad?

## Concepts or Examples

- ☐ Union
- ☐ Union-management relations
- ☐ Reactions to unions
- ☐ Attitudes toward unions
- ☐ Attitudes toward management
- ☐ Union representation election

## Analysis

_____

_____

_____

_____

_____

_____

## Personal Reactions

_____

_____

_____

_____

_____

# The Efficiency Expert (I)

Color, 1992
Running Time: 1 hour, 37 minutes
Rating: PG
Director: Mark Joffe
Distributor: *Paramount Home Video*

Balls Moccasin Company in Spotswood, Australia is losing money. A company interested in acquiring it sends a consultant to assess its condition and help improve operations. The company's president has sold assets over the years to cover its losses. Set in 1960s Australia, this film released in Australia and some other countries as *Spotswood* (Craddock 2002, 247). The following pages discuss other scenes that show different phases of organizational change.

## Scenes

- **DVD: Not available**
- **VHS: (Start: 0:10:14 — Stop: 0:20:57 — 11 minutes)**

Four scenes at different places in *The Efficiency Expert* show different aspects of organizational change processes. View each set in sequence to develop an understanding of the dynamics of these processes.

The first scenes start early in the film toward the end of the opening credits. Two cars enter the Balls Moccasin factory grounds. Consultant Errol Wallace (Sir Anthony Hopkins) arrives for his first meeting with the company's president, Mr. Ball (Alwyn Kurts). The scenes end after someone calls to Wallace. The film cuts to Cary (Ben Mendelsohn) and Wendy (Toni Collette) wheeling their bicycles across a bridge.

## What to Watch for and Ask Yourself

- What role does consultant Wallace expect to play in the planned change of Balls Moccasin Company?
- Which phase of the planned change process do these scenes show?
- How would you characterize Wallace's view of this company's management?

## Concepts or Examples

☐ Planned organizational change

☐ Change agent

☐ Readiness for change

☐ Diagnosing the present state of an organization

☐ Phases of planned change

## Analysis

_____

_____

_____

_____

_____

_____

## Personal Reactions

_____

_____

_____

_____

_____

# The Efficiency Expert (II)

For distributor information and a film description, see page 86. Other scene descriptions appear on pages 86, 90, and 92.

## Scenes

- **DVD: Not available**
- **VHS: (Start: 0:33:45 — Stop: 0:38:01 — 5 minutes)**

The second scenes start with a shot of a left-handed person (Cary, Ben Mendelsohn) signing a letter. They follow Cary's aborted effort to leave a note for Cheryl Ball (Rebecca Rigg) at her home. Both the Ball's dog and a thunderstorm chase him up a tree. The scenes end after Errol Wallace (Sir Anthony Hopkins) calls to Cary and asks him to go with him. The film cuts to a store window's display of Ball's moccasins.

## What to Watch for and Ask Yourself

- What stage of planned organizational change do these scenes show?
- What specific changes does Mr. Wallace recommend?
- How will employees react to the proposed change?

## Concepts or Examples

☐ Intervention(s)

☐ Planned organizational change

☐ Potential resistance to change

☐ Change agent

☐ Reaction to change

## Analysis

_____

_____

_____

_____

_____

## Personal Reactions

_____

_____

_____

_____

# The Efficiency Expert (III)

For distributor information and a film description, see page 86. Other scene descriptions appear on pages 86, 88, and 92.

## Scenes

- **DVD: Not available**
- **VHS: (Start: 0:53:07 — Stop: 0:57:25 — 4 minutes)**

The third scenes open on a Balls Moccasins sign on a car door. They follow Kim's (Russell Crowe) jealous rage against Cary (Ben Mendelsohn). These scenes end after Cary examines his flat bicycle tire. The film cuts to a worker protest march.

## What to Watch for and Ask Yourself

- What are the effects of Mr. Wallace's (Sir Anthony Hopkins) change efforts?
- What information could Wallace and Mr. Ball (Alwyn Kurts) learn from employee reactions to the changes?
- How could the consultant and management have reduced resistance to change?

## Concepts or Examples

☐ Organizational change effects

☐ Organizational change

☐ Change agent

☐ Reaction to change

☐ Resistance to change

☐ Information from resistance

☐ Reducing resistance to change

## Analysis

_____

_____

_____

_____

_____

## Personal Reactions

_____

_____

_____

_____

_____

_____

# The Efficiency Expert (IV)

For distributor information and a film description, see page 86. Other scene descriptions appear on pages 86, 88, and 90.

## Scenes

- **DVD: Not available**
- **VHS: (Start: 1:19:43 — Stop: 1:24:53 — 5 minutes)**

The final scenes begin with a shot of a cocktail party. The camera pans left to Errol Wallace (Sir Anthony Hopkins) standing against a wall with a drink in his hand. These scenes follow the brief scene of Cary (Ben Mendelsohn) preparing to go out for the evening and saying goodnight to his family. They end after Wallace and Mr. Ball (Alwyn Kurts) toast each other on the porch of Mr. Ball's home. The film cuts to a movie theater interior. Cary enters and walks down the aisle. There is a brief intercut scene of Cary talking to Cheryl Ball (Rebecca Rigg) in the theater lobby. The word "pissed" is Australian (and British) slang for being drunk.

## What to Watch for and Ask Yourself

- What prompted the change in Mr. Wallace's approach to the company?
- Identify the major elements of Wallace's proposed changes. Can they have strong effects on Balls Moccasin employees' behavior?
- What are your predictions for the change? Success? Failure?

## Concepts or Examples

☐ Organizational change effects     ☐ Incentives

☐ Organizational change     ☐ Resistance to change

☐ Change agent     ☐ Employee involvement

## Analysis

_____

_____

_____

_____

_____

## Personal Reactions

_____

_____

_____

_____

# The Jetsons: First Episodes

Color, 1989
Running Time: 1 hour, 30 minutes
Rating: NR
Director: William Hanna, Joseph Barbera
Distributor: *Hanna-Barbera Home Video*

This collection of four early Jetsons episodes features the arrival of Rosie the Robot and introduces the Jetson family members: George Jetson, his wife Jane, daughter Judy, and "his boy" Elroy. One episode shows Astro, the Jetson family dog, coming home with Elroy for the first time. These episodes originally aired in 1962. Many technologies in these episodes exist today or will exist soon.

## Scenes

- **DVD: Not available**
- **VHS: (Start: 0:01:28 — Stop: 0:13:12 — 12 minutes)**

This is the first episode on the videotape. The scenes start with the title screen, "Rosie the Robot." They end after George Jetson parks his saucer on his apartment building roof. He says, "I hate these compact saucers" as he walks to his apartment.

## What to Watch for and Ask Yourself

- Which technologies shown in these scenes exist today?
- Which technologies will exist in the near future?
- Which technologies are still fantasies?

## Concepts or Examples

☐ Video technology          ☐ Household technology

☐ Transportation technology ☐ Audio technology

☐ Communication technology

## Analysis

_____

_____

_____

_____

_____

_____

## Personal Reactions

_____

_____

_____

_____

# Bibliography

Allbritton, D. W., and Gerrig, R. J. 1991. Participatory Responses in Prose Understanding. *Journal of Memory and Language* 30: 603–626.

Andrew, D. 1984. *Concepts in Film Theory*. New York: Oxford University Press, Inc.

Arnheim, R. 1957. *Film as Art*. Berkeley, CA: University of California Press.

Carroll, N. 1985. The Power of Movies. *Daedalus* 114: 79–103.

Cooper, D. E. 1986. *Metaphor*. Oxford, England: Basil Blackwell.

Craddock, J., ed. 2002. *VideoHound's Golden Movie Retriever*. Farmington Hills, MI: The Gale Group, Inc.

Feinberg, L. 1967. *Introduction to Satire*. Ames, IA: Iowa State University Press.

Fowler, G. A. 2002. Hollywood Ending: Stapler Becomes a Star. *The Wall Street Journal* (2 July): B1, B4.

Germain, D. 2002. 'Casablanca' Top Romance Film: Institute Picks 100 Best Love Stories. *The Associated Press*. As the story appeared in the *Albuquerque Journal*. (12 June): C13.

Gerrig, R. J., and Prentice, D. A. 1996. Notes on Audience Response. In *Post-Theory: Reconstructing Film Studies*, D. Bordwell and N. Carroll, eds., Ch. 18. Madison, WI: University of Wisconsin Press.

Griffin, D. 1994. *Satire: a Critical Reintroduction*. Lexington, KY: University Press of Kentucky.

Hawkes, T. 1972. *Metaphor*. London: Methuen.

Jurkiewicz, K. 1990. Using Film in the Humanities Classroom: The Case of *Metropolis*. *English Journal* 79: 47–50.

Kracauer, S. 1973. *Theory of Film: The Redemption of Physical Reality*. New York: Oxford University Press.

Maltin, L., ed. 2002. *Leonard Maltin's Movie & Video Guide, 2003 Edition*. New York: SIGNET.

Martin, M., and Porter, M., eds. 2002. *Video & DVD Guide 2003*. New York: Ballantine Books.

Mooij, J. J. A. 1976. *A Study of Metaphor: On the Nature of Metaphorical Expressions, with Special References to their Reference*. Amsterdam: North-Holland Publishing Co.

Nowell-Smith, G., ed. 1996. *The Oxford History of World Cinema*. Oxford: Oxford University Press.

Peske, N., and B. West. 1999. *Cinematherapy: The Girl's Guide to Movies for Every Mood*. New York: Dell.

Proctor II, R. F., and Adler, R. B. 1991. Teaching Interpersonal Communication With Feature Films. *Communication Education* 40: 393–400.

Stadler, H. A. 1990. Film As Experience: Phenomenological Concepts in Cinema and Television Studies. *Quarterly Review of Film and Video* 12: 37–50.

Test, G. A. 1991. *Satire: Spirit and Art*. Tampa, FL: University of South Florida Press.

Wolensky, R. P., ed. 1982. *Using Films in Sociology Courses: Guidelines and Reviews*. Washington, DC: American Sociological Association.

Zorn, T. F. 1991. Willy Loman's Lesson: Teaching Identity Management with *Death of a Salesman*. *Communication Education* 40: 219–224.

# Index